The Best (& Worst) Jobs in
ANCIENT ROME

Clive Gifford

Published in paperback in 2017 by Wayland

Copyright © Hodder and Stoughton, 2017

Editor: Nicola Edwards

Designer: Rocket Design (East Anglia Ltd)

Illustrations by Alex Paterson

Dewey number: 331.7'00937–dc23

ISBN: 978 1 5263 0030 0

Library eBook ISBN: 978 0 7502 8745 6

10 9 8 7 6 5 4 3 2 1

Wayland, an imprint of

Hachette Children's Group

Part of Hodder and Stoughton

Carmelite House

50 Victoria Embankment

London EC4Y 0DZ

An Hachette UK Company

www.hachette.co.uk

www.hachettechildrens.co.uk

Printed and bound in China

All photographs supplied by
The Art Archive (www.art-archive.com)
except for pp 2(b), 5, 9, 22(b), 26 (both),
27 (both), 28 Shutterstock.com

CONTENTS

THE JOB MARKET
IN ANCIENT ROME

So, you're looking for a job in the mighty Ancient Roman Empire? Excellent!

According to legend, Rome was founded as a settlement in 753 BCE and was ruled for over 200 years by foreign powers until it became a republic and started expanding aggressively. In the first century CE, Rome gained its first emperor, Augustus, and by the end of that century held an enormous empire with the city of Rome at its centre. There, successive rulers built many mighty monuments honouring themselves, the victories of the powerful Roman army or the many gods the Romans worshipped.

Roman lands

BRITAIN

GERMANY

ASIA

EUROPE

FRANCE

SPAIN

ITALY

Mediterranean Sea

ARABIA

EGYPT

The Roman Empire at its peak under Emperor Trajan (53-117 CE) covered around 6.5 million square kilometres. It included much of Europe, North Africa and parts of the Middle East.

Rome was the biggest city in the world at that time and was home to over a million people. So, you can bet there were plenty of jobs around – from butchers and market traders to cooks, engineers and doctors. Many poor people, though, struggled to make a living. Some were forced to take truly unpleasant jobs, from scraping the dirt off people's bodies to finding employment as a Stercorarius. These workers would travel in a cart to people's houses and collect all the human waste, which they would take and sell to farms as fertilizer. Pooh!

To see what other smelly jobs might be open to you in the Roman world, and to find out which jobs were the best and the worst, read on…

Work began on building Rome's Colosseum in 70-72 CE. The magnificent amphitheatre could seat as many as 60,000 people.

ODD JOB

CURSE TABLET MAKER

Inscribing curses onto thin, rolled sheets of lead or an alloy of lead and tin was big business in the Roman era. A customer would pay a curse tablet maker to write out a curse against someone who had wronged them and then either bury the tablet or nail it to a wall. A big haul of 130 of these tablets was found by archaeologists at the Roman baths in Bath, England. Most of the curses were aimed at thieves who stole bathers' clothes while they were using the baths!

ROMAN LEGIONARY

Fighting fit

To join the mighty Roman army and become a legionary, or basic foot soldier, you had to be a Roman citizen (although non-Romans also fought as more lower-paid auxiliaries). You needed to be fit and healthy and able to read and write. Over months of basic training, new recruits would be out in all weathers, learning battle tactics, formations, how to handle different weapons and how to march long distances carrying up to 30 kg of kit on their backs. Legionaries had to get used to wearing and caring for their segmented metal and leather armour over their tunics, using olive oil or animal fat to keep the leather greased and supple.

Soldiers had to learn how to perform sudden battle formations like this *testudo*, meaning tortoise. In the testudo, the soldiers moved together in a tight unit protected from rocks and arrows by shields held out in front and above their heads.

ODD JOB
DEAD WRONG

For soldiers who stepped out of line, punishments could be brutal – from not being fed to beatings and worst of all, decimation. This was reserved for cowardice in battle and involved forcing the men in the offending cohort to draw lots with one in every ten men executed.

Forts or garrisons were set up across the Roman Empire. This mosaic from 80 BCE shows legionaries stationed in Egypt.

Long-term employment

Legionaries were paid relatively well, above the rate of craftsmen, for example, but had to sign up for long-term service of between 20 and 25 years. At the end of their service, they were paid a pension from Rome that might be as much as 12 years' pay, or were granted a gift of land to settle down and farm. In service, it wasn't all invading and battling. In between military campaigns, Roman legionaries were rarely idle and were put to work guarding territory, constructing forts or building roads.

A legionary was usually armed with both a *pilum* (javelin) with a sharp, barbed point, a dagger and a *gladius* – a sword with a blade around 60 cm long held in the right hand. In their left, they held a stout wooden and leather shield with an iron rim.

WORK MATES

CENTURION: Each legionary lived, marched and battled together as part of a unit of eight called a contubernium. Ten of these units formed a century, led by a senior soldier called a centurion. They were paid many times that of a legionary. Some centurions rose to command a cohort made up of six centuries.

JOB VERDICT

An excellent choice if you are fit and don't have another trade, as becoming a Roman legionary guaranteed you food and work. There's also the prospect of promotion if you survive many military campaigns.

FULLER

Tub trampling

A fuller or fullo washed other people's dirty, stained togas, tunics, cloth and other clothing. These clothes were often soaked in tubs in a stall or niche in which the fuller stood, trampling the clothes with their bare feet for long periods. What was worse was what the tub was filled with – water and large quantities of human and animal urine! The ammonia in the urine acted as a cleaning agent on the clothing stains. After a good long wash, the items would then be rinsed and hung over a wooden or basketwork frame to dry. Woollen clothing would often be carded or brushed afterwards to plump it up.

JOB VACANCY
Start date: 100 CE

- ARE YOU A NEAT FREAK?
- DO YOU HAVE PLENTY OF ENERGY AND ENOUGH STAMINA TO RUN ON THE SPOT ALL DAY LONG?

ODD JOB

PEE PENALTY

The Roman historian Suetonius wrote that during the reign of Roman emperor Vespasian a tax was put on urine which had to be paid by fullers!

JOB VERDICT

The pay isn't great, the conditions far from ideal, but you might get your own cleaning done for free.

A fuller stands in his stall and tramples cloth with his feet. Fullers were responsible for the condition of the clothes and could be punished if they damaged any.

THERMAE WORKER

Some like it hot

Most Romans didn't have places to bathe at home so came to large, public baths known as thermae. As a worker at a thermae, you may get a hot, heavy lifting job, constantly stoking the furnaces below the baths with firewood so that the heat from the furnaces could both heat water and send hot air rising up through parts of the building. Alternatively, you might be at work cleaning the bathers but you'd have no soap to work with. Instead, you would rub and massage people's skin with olive oil and then scrape all the oil, dirt and grime off with a long blade called a strigil. Urgh!

At a Roman baths, people would spend long parts of the day moving from hot pools and rooms to the frigidarium, usually the largest and coldest pool at the baths, to cool down.

JOB VERDICT

Not the most pleasant job in ancient Rome, but at least you'd be warm... all the time!

SLAVE TRADER

Every year, thousands of slaves were bought and sold throughout the Roman Empire. Slave traders travelled widely, often trailing a Roman army, waiting eagerly for a battle. If the Romans were victorious, they might capture many slaves, some of which the trader might buy. Traders also travelled to well-known slave markets and ports at Delos and Ephesus, for example, to buy slaves from pirates or other traders. They would then transport them to towns and cities across the Roman world where there was demand for the cheap labour slaves provided.

This Roman artwork depicts three tied-up slaves from North Africa. The Roman Emperor Augustus imposed a tax on the sale of slaves that traders had to pay to Rome.

JOB VERDICT

You may be shunned and distrusted by many in Roman society because of your job, but if you kept buying and selling slaves at a profit then you could become rich.

SLAVE

Slaves' tasks were varied depending on who their owners were. Thousands of slaves were put to work on large farms held by Romans in Spain and France. Thousands more, many of them young boys, worked in crippling conditions in silver mines. Those who were domestic slaves, cooking and cleaning Roman homes, worked in better conditions, although the work could be hard and boring. The Romans admired the ancient Greeks and educated Greek men who were enslaved were often put to work as teachers or tutors.

WORK MATES

LITTER BEARER: Some strong and fit male slaves had to work as lecticarii or litter bearers. A litter was a carriage inside which a wealthy Roman sat or lay while four slaves each holding a pole carried it up and down the hills of Rome. It was absolutely backbreaking work.

JOB VERDICT

Variable. Prospects range from not too bad (working for a kind, wealthy household) to dreadful (if you were forced down the silver mines). Your only hope was to be able to buy or earn your freedom.

EMPEROR

In charge

Rome and its empire was ruled by a senate, a group of powerful men, until the first century CE. That was when the first in a long line of emperors – supreme rulers – came to power. Emperors could raise funds by imposing new taxes although some, such as Nero, chose to murder prominent Romans and seize their property as well. They could introduce new laws and many ordered large building programmes, including monuments, honouring themselves.

It goes without saying that they lived a life of luxury and had the best seat at gladiatorial games, feasts and other entertainments.

JOB VACANCY
Start date: 100 CE

- ARE YOU A ROMAN CITIZEN?
- DO YOU LIKE BEING POWERFUL, IN CONTROL, AND MAKING BIG DECISIONS?
- ARE YOU FOND OF BEING FLATTERED AND SHOWERED WITH PRAISE AND GIFTS?
- CAN YOU SPOT A PLOT AND ARE YOU RUTHLESS ENOUGH TO EXECUTE THOSE RESPONSIBLE?

ODD JOB

THE COLOUR PURPLE

Tyrian purple was a dye made from thousands of small sea snails. It was very expensive, and during his reign Nero made it a crime punishable by death for anyone other than the emperor to wear it.

A job for life

For a Roman emperor there were no elections or early retirements. So, Romans were stuck with their ruler even if he was crazy, evil or unfit to govern. This led to many plots being hatched to topple emperors and murder them. More than 40 emperors were killed, some such as Pertinax and Caligula, by members of the Praetorian Guard, the very group of trusted elite soldiers supposed to protect the emperor. To stay in office therefore, an emperor had to stamp out plots ruthlessly, often banishing close allies or having plotting members of his own family executed.

Octavian, the nephew of Julius Caesar, became the first emperor of Rome in 27 CE and was given the name Augustus. As Emperor, Augustus established a postal service and helped turn the Roman army into a professional and fearsome fighting force.

This painting shows the murder of the Roman Emperor Domitian in 96 CE.

This is a statue of Trajan, the Roman emperor who embarked on military campaigns in North Africa and Dacia (present-day Romania) and built many structures in Rome including Trajan's Forum and Trajan's Column.

JOB VERDICT

Simply the best! You'll have all the power of mighty Rome at your fingertips. Watch out for plots behind your back, though, if you don't govern the empire fairly and correctly.

COOK

Making a meal of it

Cooks were employed in many wealthy Roman homes and would shop at the local market for ingredients. Many cooks were slaves. Each day, the cook would have to prepare ingredients and cook meals using a stone hearth filled with firewood or charcoal over which they would roast or boil foods. Cooks would also use a stone or brick oven in which they regularly baked bread. The work could be hard and unrelenting with the daily risk of burns and cuts. The pressure was most intense before dinner. This meal often consisted of many dishes and courses, all of which had to be cooked in small, cramped and hot kitchens.

ODD JOB

FEAST YOUR EYES

Some feasts for the wealthiest Romans featured the strangest dishes, from peacock brains and the tongues of flamingos, to baby rabbits and even elephant's trunk! One rare delicacy was a Trojan pig — a whole pig stuffed with spiced sausages that were arranged to look like the pig's guts when it was cut open. Urgh!

A cook bakes bread in an oven in this Roman mosaic. Bread was eaten with most meals and even turned into a dessert by soaking it in milk and frying it with honey.

A Roman cook selects ingredients stored in jars in a kitchen. Many ordinary Romans living in cities could not afford a kitchen, so heated basic food over a little brazier, similar to a small barbecue, or ate out at taverns or market stalls.

Sweet and sour

The Romans used honey and fruit to sweeten their dishes and had a liking for strong herbs and spices, garlic and a smelly sauce called garum. This was the tomato ketchup of its day, but was made from the rotting intestines of fish and cooks had to put up with its overpowering smell. At least there wasn't too much washing up as most meals were eaten with the fingers.

GLADIATOR

Sent to school

Gladiators fought against each other in Roman games for the entertainment of bloodthirsty crowds in large, open-air venues called amphitheatres. With death a common outcome and severe injuries in training possible, there was always a demand for new recruits. Slaves, enemy soldiers captured in battle and criminals were all forced to join a gladiator school called a ludus. Rome had four Ludi, the largest of which – the Ludus Magnus – housed around 2,000 gladiators. A small number of gladiators were free men who choose the fighting life, while one Roman emperor, Commodus (161CE-192 CE), sometimes fought as a gladiator for fun!

L. IMPROBVM

Inside an amphitheatre the lowest seats, closest to the action, were the most expensive. Vats of strong-smelling incense masked the smell of blood and guts whilst young slave boys would rake the sand to cover up bloodstains.

Fighting chance

Led into the arena, gladiators were released and then had to battle under the eye of a referee called a summa rudis. Not all contests ended in death. Sometimes, bouts were stopped if one gladiator was seriously wounded or could not defend himself. Many contests, though, were fought to the death. Dead or dying gladiators might be dragged off using a big hook and chain, or an executioner would kill them off using a large hammer. Winning gladiators won prizes but were still slaves. Only by triumphing in a large number of bouts could a gladiator regain his freedom.

ODD JOB

MEN, WOMEN AND CHILDREN

Gladiator battles were just part of the entertainment at a Roman games. Sometimes, criminals and Christians were thrown to hungry wild animals. Even female gladiators fought on occasion while in 66 CE, Nero staged fights between women, men and children to entertain visiting ruler, King Tiridates I of Armenia.

JOB VERDICT

Potentially lethal. You would put your life on the line every time you competed. If you managed to survive many bouts, you might be set free or made a gladiator trainer. At least you got food and a home... while you lived!

PHYSICIAN

Doctor, doctor

The Romans learned much of their medicine from the ancient Greeks, and Greek doctors were particularly in demand. Many physicians trained as an apprentice to an experienced doctor or learned their trade in the Roman army where they might have to deal with some truly terrible injuries. There were no medical exams, so many people just set up as doctors and hoped to find patients. Just like the Greeks, the Romans often mixed religious rituals with physical medicine and herbal remedies.

One Roman army doctor, Pedanius Dioscorides, wrote a book listing more than 600 cures using herbs and other plants. Another Roman physician, Aulus Cornelius Celus, prescribed drinking the blood of a slain gladiator as a cure for epilepsy!

This painting shows a doctor attending to a soldier who has a wound to his thigh. Wounds were often dressed with linen bandages sometimes soaked in wine or vinegar in order to prevent infection.

JOB VACANCY
Start date: 100 CE

- DOES THE SIGHT OF BLOOD NOT BOTHER YOU AT ALL?
- DO YOU HAVE A TERRIFIC MEMORY FOR FACTS, COMPLICATED REMEDIES AND RITUALS?
- CAN YOU CONVINCE OTHERS THAT YOU'RE ABLE TO HEAL THEM?

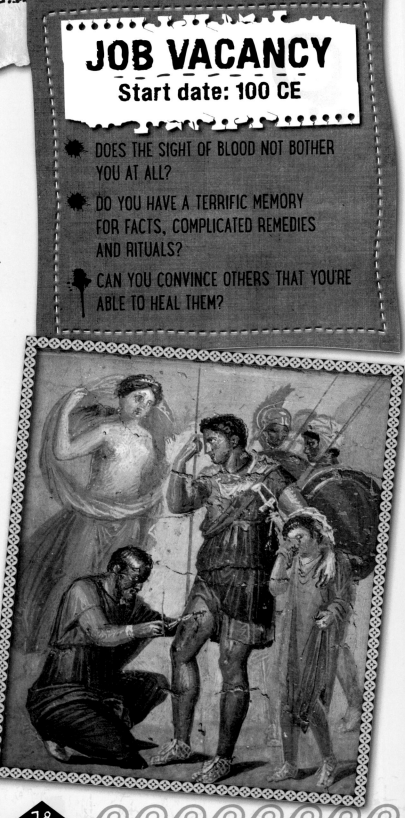

Cutting edge

Many Roman doctors would also perform surgery such as draining fluid from the body and removing arrowheads from a wound. They would quickly get used to patients struggling and screaming as there were no anaesthetics. At most, patients might be made a little drowsy by drinking some wine. Those who survived surgery had their wounds stitched with thread made from linen or flax.

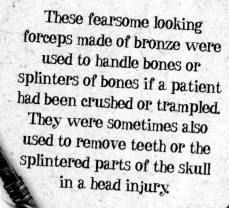

These fearsome looking forceps made of bronze were used to handle bones or splinters of bones if a patient had been crushed or trampled. They were sometimes also used to remove teeth or the splintered parts of the skull in a head injury.

Preparing remedies out of natural ingredients in an Ancient Roman pharmacy.

ODD JOB

TAX-FREE DUTY

Some doctors called *archiatri populares* treated poor patients in a Roman city for free and in return did not have to pay any tax. They could also take on wealthy patients who paid for their treatments.

JOB VERDICT

Pretty good. Although doctors didn't have the status in society that the medical profession has today, some became popular and counted generals and emperors as their patients.

TEACHER

Types of teacher

Roman teachers, known as *litterators*, taught reading, writing and the basics of Roman numbers to young students, who were all boys. Some older boys from the age of 11 or 12 went to a *Grammaticus*, where they were taught poetry, grammar and sometimes other subjects such as history, geometry and astronomy. Pupils learned and recited works of famous authors. Teachers didn't work in a dedicated school building. They often rented out a room at the back of a shop. School days could be long for teachers and pupils, often starting before dawn and extending throughout the day.

JOB VACANCY
Start date: 100 CE

● ARE YOU WELL-READ, WITH A LOVE OF LEARNING?

● CAN YOU RECALL AND RECITE LOTS OF INFORMATION FROM MEMORY?

● ARE YOU GOOD AT MAKING CHILDREN PAY ATTENTION AND PUNISHING THEM IF THEY DO NOT?

WORK MATES

PAEDAGOGUS: This adult, usually a slave owned by a wealthy Roman household, walked a boy to and from school. Often, they were well educated and might help the pupil with his lessons.

A teacher (left) instructs students as one reads from a scroll made of flattened papyrus reeds. These scrolls were expensive and rare. Some schools operated with no scrolls at all.

School fees

The most notable teachers built a reputation that allowed them to charge high fees. In 301 CE, the emperor, Diocletian set maximum rates for teachers' wages. A litterator could receive up to 50 denarii per student per month whilst a teacher of older boys could receive up to 250 denarii per pupil per month. In comparison, a barber could earn a maximum of two denarii per customer and a farm labourer up to 25 denarii a day. So, teaching could be a profitable occupation if you had a large number of students.

A Roman schoolteacher holds a ferula – a stick that was sometimes used to beat unruly school children. Slaves were used as teaching assistants and it was one of their duties to hold children down while they were beaten.

The Romans used a pointed wooden stick or stylus to write on wooden tablets covered in a layer of wax. The wax was melted and smoothed over after use so that the tablet could be used again.

JOB VERDICT

A nice, safe, indoor job for those who like books, reading and knowledge, providing you can deal with children all day.

ACTOR

It's all Greek to me

The Romans took much of their love of theatre and acting from the ancient Greeks. At first, their plays copied or adapted Greek tragedies and comedies, but over time, Roman playwrights produced their own original plays. Many were short and based on domestic life with stock characters such as the *adulescens* – the young hero – and the *pappas* – the foolish old man. These were played by actors who were known as *histriones*. At first, only men appeared on stage, but in the later centuries of the Roman Empire, female actors appeared.

Roman actors also often copied the ancient Greek tradition of wearing masks to play their characters, as this mosaic shows.

An actor might be fortunate enough to be part of a company that performed in a large stone theatre such as this one in Bosra, Syria, which could hold up to 15,000 spectators.

22

STAR TURN

Most actors weren't well known but a few found great success, such as Roscius (126–62 BCE). Born a slave, he earned enough money to buy his freedom, become famous and count politicians and generals as friends. He is said to have earned an equivalent of 1,000 denarii per performance – when a peasant might earn just a hundredth of that for a day's hard labour.

To attract people to plays, a company might use special effects such as fire, smoke, animal blood, fake heads and mechanical machines to lift and move actors about the stage.

A company of players

Actors were usually part of a company and may even have been slaves owned by the company leader. Roman audiences could be lively and thought nothing of shouting and hissing during a performance. The Romans didn't think much of acting as a job. They thought actors had poor morals partly because of the rude plays they might perform on the stage. Some Roman emperors such as Tiberius prohibited actors from mixing with important Romans or prevented Roman citizens from becoming actors.

JOB VERDICT

It was a precarious living for most actors. Plays had to be popular and pull in the crowds before the actors were paid.

CHARIOT RACER

Circus skills

Chariot racers, known as *aurigae*, were the Formula One superstars of their day. They were praised, cheered and bet on by thousands of Romans. Although chariot racers might ride and train in the countryside, their real workplace was at a circus – a large, open-air venue in the middle of which lay the oval-shaped track with a long barrier called a *spina*. The largest circus of all was the Circus Maximus which, at 621 m, was longer than six football pitches and had seating for over 150,000 spectators.

This re-enactment of a Roman chariot race features two-horse *biga* chariots. The driver wound the leather reins around his hands or waist and carried a sharp knife to cut the reins should he fall from the chariot.

A racer handles a four horse *quadriga* chariot. The chariot itself weighed less than 30 kg and the chariot racer stood on a small platform over the axle that joined the chariot's two wheels. Speeds on the straight may have been as high as 50 km/h.

Race time

Races were preceded by processions and entertainment to build excitement among the crowd. Each chariot racer would wear the racing colours of one of the four racing stables, known as *factiones*: red, white, blue or green. There would be up to 12 chariots thundering around the track, usually in races lasting seven laps. Charioteers had to balance on the tiny wooden platform and shift their body suddenly while pulling hard on the reins to get around corners. Crashes were common as were falls and charioteers being dragged along by their own horses or trampled by a rival racer's. As a result, many racers died young or suffered severe injuries.

This mosaic from Sicily shows a trumpeter (left) and an official holding an olive branch and small wreath to present to the race winner. Prize money was also given and at big races, it could be huge.

ODD JOB

CHAMPION RACER

Gaius Appuleius Diocles was a phenomenally successful chariot racer who was said to have won over 1,400 *quadriga* races during his long career. He is recorded as winning around 9 million denarii — equal to more than £8 billion today!

JOB VERDICT

A high-risk job with the threat of death or injury always present. But for those who survived and were frequent winners, there was great acclaim and wealth to be won.

ENGINEER

Engineering expertise

The Romans were highly skilful and resourceful engineers who solved many problems as they constructed astonishing structures, some of which survive to this day. Many engineers came from wealthy families who could afford to pay for them to be educated for many years. Some engineers became apprentices to experienced engineers and architects. Others learned their trade in the Roman army, where they might have helped to survey and organize road building as well as constructing bridges to cross water when a new territory was invaded. Engineers in Julius Caesar's army, for example, are said to have constructed a large bridge, spanning more than 140 m, over the River Rhine in just ten days.

The Romans used lots of stone and brick arch shapes to build aqueducts, which carried water from distant sources to their towns and cities.

Roman engineers were expert at designing and working with concrete. The concrete dome of the Pantheon in Rome was constructed over 1,900 years ago and is still in place today.

Material matters

Engineers needed to thoroughly understand the materials with which their builders would be working, organize the building project and command hundreds, sometimes thousands, of workers. The Romans developed a particularly strong form of concrete that used *pozzolana* – a type of volcanic ash – amongst its ingredients. Many Roman buildings were made of concrete and stone, while scaffolding towers around partly-built structures were made of wood.

Roman engineers developed amazing polypastos cranes which were powered by people moving round a treadmill. These giant wooden cranes could lift heavy loads up to 6,000 kg.

WORK MATES

ROAD BUILDERS: Roman engineers helped build thousands of kilometres of straight, well-drained roads throughout the empire which allowed its armies and messengers to travel quickly. The roads were constructed of many different layers topped with hardwearing stone slabs.

JOB VERDICT

Very good. Being a successful engineer was a high status job in Roman society and many were popular with wealthy and powerful leaders in Rome... as long as their building projects continued to go well.

MARKET TRADER

The market place

Every Roman town and city had at least one forum, an area that offered both a place to meet and a lively market. In Rome, there were large, dedicated markets including the giant Trajan's Market which contained over 150 shops around its perimeter. Everything from food, oil and wine to clothes, crafts and tools were sold at market. Each seller was under pressure to make frequent sales to make a living. This pressure forced some traders to sell poor goods such as stale bread or sour wine. If they did, there was a good chance that they would be caught by market officials called aediles who could impose very heavy fines.

JOB VACANCY
Start date: 100 CE

- ARE YOU GOOD AT MATHS AND ABLE TO JUGGLE SUMS IN YOUR HEAD?
- CAN YOU SELL, SELL, SELL AND CONVINCE DITHERING CUSTOMERS TO PART WITH THEIR CASH?

The surviving remains of Trajan's Market in Rome. Designed by the architect, Apollodorus, the market buildings were constructed from brick and concrete.

JOB VERDICT

Not bad if you managed to sell well and didn't get into heavy debt with money lenders.

BUTCHER

Chopping shop

Out in the countryside, many people butchered their own livestock. In towns butchers operated from a shop, with the filleting of animals done in the back and sales conducted at the front. There weren't as many butchers as there were shops for other foodstuffs because meat was an expensive luxury. Pork is believed to be the most common meat although beef, boar and wild rabbits and hares were also sold. Operating in a warm climate meant that meat had to be sold quickly before it spoiled.

A tympanum is a sign found over a doorway that shows symbols of the butcher's tools, including a cleaving axe and two knives.

This Roman mosaic shows a butcher cutting up a pig.

QUIZ

What job would most suit you in ancient Rome? Answer the questions below, then turn the book upside down to read which job might be the right one for you.

Questions

1 **Are you strong, fearless and up for a fight?**

a) Absolutely. I like nothing more than a confrontation.

b) No, I am all for a peaceful life, but I don't mind the sight of blood.

c) I am prepared to fight if necessary, but I prefer to get others to do my fighting for me.

2 **Can you read and write well and hold lots of information in your memory?**

a) I can remember a few instructions and orders but prefer doing to reading.

b) I can read and remember lots of things.

c) Yes, I think I remember things well and can give speeches.

3 **Are you ambitious and keen on gaining power and status?**

a) Not particularly, although I wouldn't mind being promoted after a few years.

b) I am not that interested in rising up through the ranks.

c) Absolutely. I want to be important and stand out from the crowd.

4 **Are you practical and good with your hands?**

a) I am fairly practical, can build things and carry loads.

b) Yes, I am good with my hands, especially doing precise work.

c) Not particularly, I prefer others to make things for me.

Answers

Mostly As
It sounds like you may be cut out to be a gladiator or possibly a legionary in the Roman army.

Mostly Bs
You might be best advised to consider a career in the Roman era as a doctor, or just possibly, a teacher.

Mostly Cs
You might want to set your sights on the very top job of Emperor of Rome!

Glossary

amphitheatre A venue similar to a stadium where Romans went to watch gladiators fighting and other entertainments.

anaesthetics Substances that reduce the amount of pain a living thing feels.

aqueduct A system of pipes and channels that brings clean water to towns and cities.

archaeologists People who study ancient peoples and civilizations and unearth historic artefacts.

denarii Small silver Roman coins that were used throughout the Roman world from around 210BCE to 300CE.

filleting To remove the bones from a fish or animal or joint of meat.

forum An open space in the middle of a town for markets and meeting people. The forum was often surrounded by public buildings such as law courts.

gladiator A person, often a slave, trained to fight other gladiators or animals in amphitheatres.

mosaic A picture or decorative design made of small coloured pieces of stone or tile.

Praetorian Guard A force of bodyguards organized to protect a Roman emperor.

taxes Money or items taken by the government from people to pay for army and defence, building roads and public buildings.

toga A long, loose piece of clothing wrapped around the body of some ancient Romans.

Further Information

Books

The History Detective Investigates: Ancient Rome – Rachel Minay (Wayland, 2014)

Facts At Your Fingertips: Ancient Rome (Wayland, 2009)

At Home With The Romans – Tim Cooke (Wayland 2014)

Roman Life: Work – Nicola Barber (Wayland, 2014)

Websites

http://www.pbs.org/empires/romans/index.html
Learn more about the Roman Empire and its emperors at this atmospheric website brought to you by PBS.

http://www.bbc.co.uk/history/ancient/romans/
Lots of fascinating in-depth details about gladiators, emperors and ancient Roman life at this BBC website.

http://romereborn.frischerconsulting.com/gallery-current.php
Amazing 3D views of what the city of Rome might have looked at during the height of the Roman Empire.

http://www.pbs.org/wgbh/nova/lostempires/roman
Learn about aqueducts and what it would be like to spend a day at an ancient Roman baths at this informative website.

INDEX